PUZZLE book of ANIMALS

Tons of **COOL ACTIVITIES** and **FUN FACTS**

NATIONAL GEOGRAPHIC
WASHINGTON, D.C.

CONTENTS

WILD CATS..........6

Think you've got what it takes to tackle these wild puzzles? Test your talents with fun crosswords, sudoku, and more! Need a little help? No worries, you'll find solutions in the back of the book.

IN THE RAINFOREST ...16

SWAMPS AND WETLANDS ... 26

WILD CATS

Are you brave enough for FUN FACTS and PUZZLES about BIG CATS? Read on to find out more.

A lion's **MIGHTY ROAR** is so **LOUD** it can be heard up to **5 MILES (8 km) AWAY!**

CROSSWORDS

Fill in the crosswords by solving the cryptic clues below.

Can you work out the big cat code word using the letters in the shaded squares?

ACROSS
1 Small wildflowers with white petals
6 Tiny piece of bread
7 Of great significance
8 Brother of your father or mother
9 A leafy green vegetable

DOWN
1 Hard
2 Not right
3 Hot dog or kielbasa
4 Material; anagram of "cuts beans"
5 Normal and usual

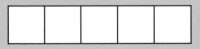

EVERY TIGER in the **WORLD** has a completely **UNIQUE STRIPE PATTERN.**

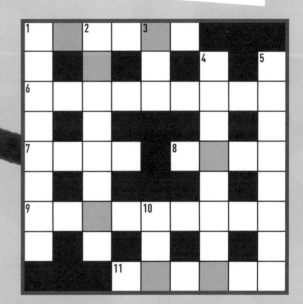

PANTHERS are actually black **LEOPARDS** or **JAGUARS.** They still have **SPOTS,** but they're **HARDER TO SEE.**

ACROSS
1 Small red fruit with a hard stone
6 Nine plus eight
7 Birds of prey that hoot
8 Create
9 The opposite of cheap
11 Road

DOWN
1 Person who buys something in a shop
2 You put a letter in this before posting it
3 Sprint
4 A sister or uncle, for instance
5 Excite the curiosity of someone
10 Food for a squirrel

SUDOKU

Help the cats solve the sudoku.
Fill in the blank squares
so that numbers 1 to 6
appear once in each row,
column, and 3x2 box.

LYNX are **STEALTHY, MYSTERIOUS CREATURES** and are rarely **SEEN BY HUMANS.**

		5			4
				6	3
2	3		6	4	
		6	1	3	2
1	2				
			4		

Unlike most cats, **JAGUARS LIKE WATER** and are **VERY GOOD SWIMMERS.**

WORD SEARCHES

Can you find the big cat words?

Search left to right and up and down to find the words listed in the boxes below.

cheetah

jaguar

leopard

lion

panther

puma

roar

spots

stripes

tiger

LEOPARDS are **GREAT CLIMBERS,** and sometimes like to **REST HIGH UP IN THE TREES.**

e	k	e	s	u	w	g	f	e	s
x	d	a	g	j	a	g	u	a	r
o	a	w	s	p	s	p	o	t	s
o	p	u	m	a	t	r	l	r	e
y	l	i	o	n	r	a	e	e	l
u	a	k	t	t	i	r	o	a	r
z	z	k	o	h	p	t	p	s	s
s	v	c	h	e	e	t	a	h	a
t	i	g	e	r	s	a	r	w	e
a	x	b	p	l	j	i	d	c	s

SNOW LEOPARDS have **BIG, WIDE, FURRY FEET** that act like **NATURAL SNOWSHOES.**

```
w  a  u  x  l  m  u  p  b  g
r  q  c  o  u  g  a  r  s  h
a  g  a  t  a  t  s  p  g  g
o  p  r  e  d  a  t  o  r  t
p  r  n  e  s  c  e  u  i  s
t  e  i  t  o  l  a  n  c  a
i  y  v  h  w  a  l  c  z  r
t  l  o  f  m  w  t  e  m  o
c  y  r  u  d  s  h  i  h  r
f  i  e  r  c  e  a  w  i  a
```

carnivore

claws

cougar

fierce

fur

pounce

predator

prey

stealth

teeth

QUIZ WHIZ

Do you know the answers to the big cat questions below?

1. Which big cat is mistakenly known as the "king of the jungle"?
   a. Elephant
   b. Lion
   c. Hyena

2. Leopards are known for their:
   a. Bark
   b. Stripes
   c. Spots

3. Which big cat is also known as a mountain lion?
   a. Puma
   b. Donkey
   c. Ocelot

4. Which is the fastest animal on land?
   a. Lion
   b. Cheetah
   c. Tiger

5. Why do snow leopards have very large paws?
   a. To jump higher
   b. To use tools
   c. To help distribute their weight when walking on snow

6. If a male lion and female tiger breed they produce a:
   a. Tigeron
   b. Liger
   c. Lionger

7. Which is the largest cat species?
   a. Lion
   b. Jaguar
   c. Tiger

8. Lions live together in a group known as a:
   a. Team
   b. Flock
   c. Pride

9. A jaguar's preferred habitat is:
   a. Dense rainforest
   b. Desert
   c. Sea

10. An adult lion's roar can be heard:
    a. 55 yards (50 m) away
    b. 5 miles (8 km) away
    c. 50 miles (80 km) away

CHEETAH ▶

MAZE

Help the lioness around the maze to find her cub.

WORD WHEELS

Can you unscramble the big cats in the two word wheels?

IN THE RAINFOREST

Swing through this chapter to find **FUN FACTS** and **PUZZLES** from the rainforest.

Look familiar? The **ORANGUTAN** is one of our **CLOSEST RELATIVES**— we have nearly **97%** of the **SAME DNA!**

CROSSWORDS

Fill in the crosswords by solving the cryptic clues below.

Can you work out the rainforest animal code word using the letters in the shaded squares?

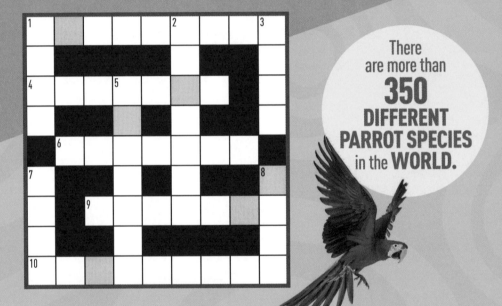

There are more than **350** DIFFERENT **PARROT SPECIES** in the **WORLD.**

ACROSS
1 The first meal of the day
4 You have this after dinner
6 Place where bees live
9 Sour liquid in salad dressing
10 Say you're sorry

DOWN
1 People sleep in these
2 Pardon; excuse
3 The end parts of the feet
5 Better or more important than other things
7 Large American wild cat also known as a cougar
8 A woody plant such as an oak

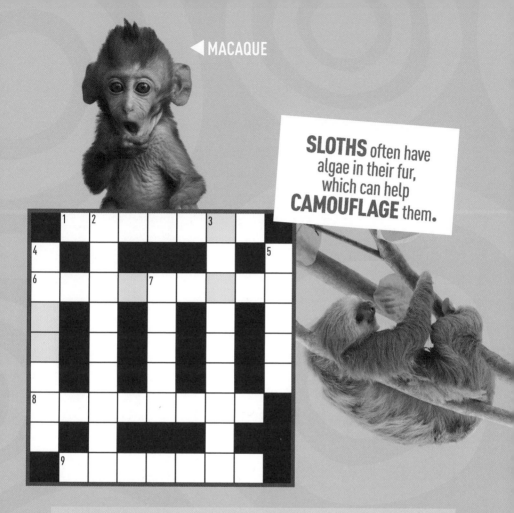

◀ MACAQUE

SLOTHS often have algae in their fur, which can help **CAMOUFLAGE** them.

ACROSS
1 Orange vegetables
6 Not liked
8 The person who lives next door to you
9 One more

DOWN
2 Creature like a frog or toad
3 Device used to study stars
4 The opposite of pulling
5 Compose on paper
7 Juicy yellowish pink fruit

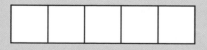

SUDOKU

Help the rainforest animals solve the sudoku.
Fill in the blank squares so that numbers 1 to 6
appear once in each row, column, and 3x2 box.

3	6	1	4	2	5
2	4	5	6	1	3
5	1	3	2	4	6
6	2	4	3	5	1
1	3	2	5	6	4
4	5	6	1	3	2

A TREE FROG'S NEON COLORS may **SHOCK** and **CONFUSE** predators, allowing the frog to **JUMP AWAY.**

The **WORLD** is home to over **10,000 SPECIES** of ANTS.

WORD SEARCHES

Can you find the rainforest words?

Search left to right and up and down to find the words listed in the boxes below.

bush baby
caiman
chameleon
cobra
macaw

ocelot
orangutan
panther
piranha
tapir

One of the **MOST COLORFUL** types of **TOUCAN** is the **KEEL-BILLED,** or **"RAINBOW-BILLED,"** toucan.

a	g	s	c	o	c	e	l	o	t
q	o	t	p	a	n	t	h	e	r
c	a	i	m	a	n	i	l	e	p
b	u	s	h	b	a	b	y	j	i
r	p	a	y	e	t	a	p	i	r
t	s	a	y	n	r	b	x	t	a
t	o	r	a	n	g	u	t	a	n
r	l	m	a	c	a	w	s	z	h
t	o	j	a	v	c	o	b	r	a
x	c	h	a	m	e	l	e	o	n

i	m	b	a	t	o	u	c	a	n
l	l	a	x	p	h	m	h	g	e
m	v	a	e	y	i	p	i	o	n
q	y	o	l	t	x	x	m	r	t
q	t	p	q	h	u	o	p	i	d
a	n	a	c	o	n	d	a	l	u
s	l	r	f	n	a	r	n	l	o
y	f	r	o	g	a	r	z	a	a
s	l	o	t	h	i	s	e	i	p
i	s	t	f	o	e	i	e	p	s

anaconda

bat

chimpanzee

frog

gorilla

parrot

python

sloth

toucan

GREEN ANACONDAS are the **LARGEST** and **HEAVIEST SNAKES** in the world.

SPOT THE DIFFERENCE

Compare the two images of the tree frog. Can you spot the five differences between the images?

SWAMPS AND WETLANDS

Make your way through this section to discover **FUN FACTS** and **PUZZLES** about wetland critters.

CROCODILES as we know them today have been on **EARTH** for about **80 MILLION YEARS!**

CROSSWORDS

Fill in the crosswords by solving the cryptic clues below.

Can you work out the swamp animal code word using the letters in the shaded squares?

In 1935, **3,500 CANE TOADS** were released in **AUSTRALIA**—now there are over **200 MILLION.**

ACROSS
1 Straight; credit (anagram)
5 A young tiger
7 Sprinted
8 You might spread this on toast
9 Organ with a pupil and iris
10 Animal that barks
11 Opposite of oldest

DOWN
1 Last month of the year
2 Simple musical instrument
3 Shape with three sides
4 Global computer network you use to visit websites
6 Facial hair

GREEN TREE FROG ▶

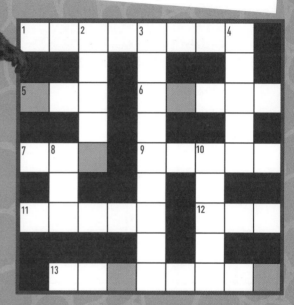

RIVER OTTERS are very playful. They love to slide down **MUDDY** or **SNOWY HILLS** for **FUN.**

ACROSS
1 Mistakes
5 Weird or strange; not even
6 Water vapor
7 Substancee all around you
9 A flat surface
11 Birds that honk
12 How old you are
13 Way in

DOWN
2 Beneath
3 Vanish from sight
4 A dirty mark on clothes
8 Frozen water
10 Once more

SUDOKU

Help the swamp animals solve the sudoku.

Fill in the blank squares so that numbers 1 to 6 appear once in each row, column, and 3x2 box.

			6		2
		3		4	
4		6			3
2			1		4
3	5		4		
1		4			

HERONS are **EXPERT FISHERS**, and usually **EAT FISH** by **SWALLOWING THEM WHOLE!**

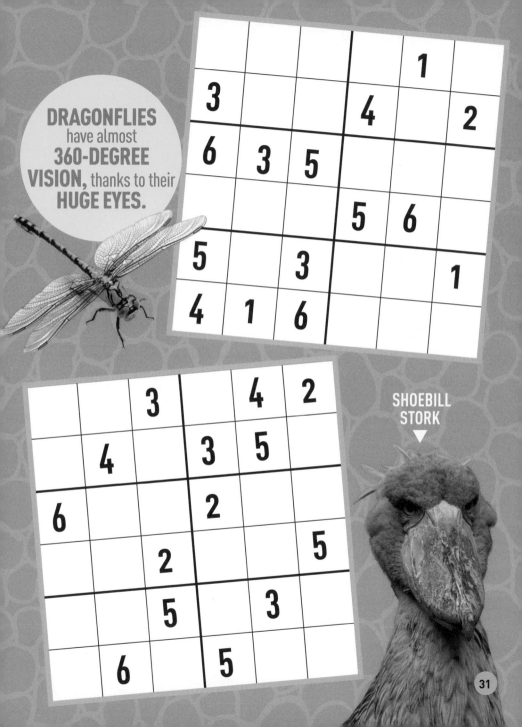

DRAGONFLIES have almost 360-DEGREE VISION, thanks to their HUGE EYES.

SHOEBILL STORK ▼

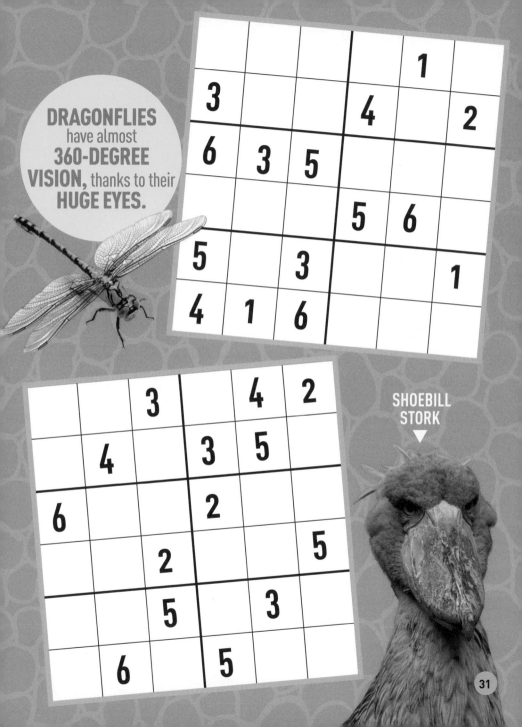

31

WORD SEARCHES

Can you find the wetlands words?

Search left to right and up and down to find the words listed in the boxes below.

crab
crane
crocodile
dragonfly
frog

lizard
marsh
otter
snake
turtle

A **BEAVER'S FUR** is **OILY** and **NATURALLY WATERPROOF,** which keeps the skin underneath **NICE AND DRY.**

l	p	u	c	r	a	n	e	h	e
o	m	a	r	s	h	r	u	d	p
j	x	m	o	n	e	l	a	r	x
t	i	a	c	a	t	c	r	a	b
u	b	b	o	k	f	r	o	g	g
z	i	v	d	e	k	e	r	o	o
d	j	l	i	z	a	r	d	n	t
v	r	d	l	a	l	l	o	f	t
u	c	b	e	t	u	r	t	l	e
p	t	w	d	g	t	s	k	y	r

FLAMINGOS are **BORN GRAY** but gradually turn pink because of a **DYE IN THE SHRIMP** that they eat.

```
l  y  a  b  u  r  t  w  c  s
m  r  d  e  h  y  b  w  r  h
a  z  u  a  e  f  l  h  a  r
n  e  c  v  r  l  a  c  y  i
g  c  k  e  o  a  c  p  f  m
r  a  s  r  n  m  k  f  i  p
o  i  i  g  a  i  b  r  s  y
v  m  l  u  i  n  e  a  h  m
e  a  l  l  i  g  a  t  o  r
u  n  t  s  q  o  r  c  q  e
```

alligator
beaver
black bear
caiman
crayfish

duck
flamingo
heron
mangrove
shrimp

SPOT THE DIFFERENCE

Compare the two images of the crocodiles.
Can you spot the five differences
between the images?

CASSIUS,
the oldest known
crocodile in the world,
is more than
**110
YEARS OLD.**

QUIZ WHIZ

Do you know the answers to the swamp and wetlands questions below?

1. Which kind of enormous snake lives in South American swamps?
   a. Anaconda
   b. Adder
   c. Grass snake

2. Which of these is a type of bird?
   a. Crane
   b. Tractor
   c. Van

3. Which of these is a type of duck?
   a. Buzzard
   b. Leotard
   c. Mallard

4. Beavers are known for:
   a. Eating meat
   b. Building dams
   c. Climbing mountains

5. Which of the following is a rodent?
   a. Newt
   b. Snail
   c. Rat

6. Which of these creatures walks sideways?
   a. Giraffe
   b. Dog
   c. Crab

7. Why do dragonflies dip their tails into water?
   a. To drink
   b. To lay eggs
   c. To test the water temperature

8. Which of these is a type of wetland?
   a. Bog
   b. Meadow
   c. Prairie

9. Which plant might you find in a pond?
   a. Water lily
   b. Cactus
   c. Rose

10. What is the larva of a frog called?
    a. Tadpole
    b. Maypole
    c. Flagpole

◄ BOA CONSTRICTOR

Help the crocodile through the maze.

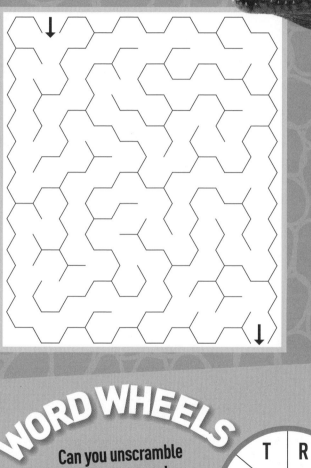

MAZE

WORD WHEELS

Can you unscramble the swamp and wetlands animals in the two word wheels?

ON SAFARI

Buckle up and keep your eyes peeled in this chapter for **FUN FACTS** and **PUZZLES** about safari animals.

MEASURING up to **20 FEET** (6 m), **GIRAFFES** are the **TALLEST ANIMALS** in the **WORLD!**

CROSSWORDS

Fill in the crosswords by solving the cryptic clues below.

Can you work out the safari animal code word using the letters in the shaded squares?

An **ELEPHANT** can be pregnant for up to **22 MONTHS** before its baby is born.

ACROSS

1 An entertainer who performs gymnastic feats
6 Slippery snake-like fish
8 Time of day before you go to bed
9 Large African ape
10 Nine plus one
11 Large cat also known as a panther

DOWN

2 Acknowledge a significant date such as your birthday
3 Large reptile
4 Shape with six sides
5 Where one finds London
7 Respond

HIPPOS can SHUT their EARS and NOSTRILS underwater and hold their breath for up to FIVE MINUTES.

◀ CHEETAH

ACROSS
1 Become less
5 Selected
7 Yellow citrus fruit
8 House made of solid snow
9 Very odd; strange
10 Animals that pull Santa's sleigh

DOWN
1 Choice or selection
2 Hot ___ : sweet cocoa drink
3 Ship that goes underwater
4 Think carefully about
6 Arm joint

SUDOKU

Help the safari animals solve the sudoku.

Fill in the blank squares so that numbers 1 to 6 appear once in each row, column, and 3x2 box.

Despite many theories, **SCIENTISTS** still aren't completely sure **WHY ZEBRAS HAVE STRIPES.**

			6		
1	4			5	
3	5		2	6	4
	6	2			5
				2	3
		3			

Puzzle 1

	3		1	6	2
			5		
1		5			3
3			4		5
		1	3		
6		3			

VULTURES are the **TRASH COLLECTORS** of the animal world, cleaning up messes by eating animals that have died.

Puzzle 2

4	1	5			
		2	4		
		4			5
	5		2		
		6	5		
5			1	2	4

RHINOCEROS

43

WORD SEARCHES

Can you find the safari words?

Search left to right and up and down to find the words listed in the boxes below.

e	j	a	c	k	a	l	s	m	g
d	r	r	w	i	l	d	d	o	g
q	r	b	x	b	k	s	j	n	s
f	h	a	o	z	g	r	t	g	o
b	y	b	o	r	o	l	p	o	s
p	e	o	l	r	p	h	o	t	t
r	n	o	y	a	i	j	c	s	r
r	a	n	t	e	l	o	p	e	i
a	g	a	z	e	l	l	e	l	c
i	m	p	a	l	a	t	q	p	h

antelope
baboon
gazelle
gorilla
hyena

impala
jackal
mongoose
ostrich
wild dog

LIONS usually only live on **GRASS PLAINS,** so they aren't really **KINGS OF THE JUNGLE** after all.

Word Search

buffalo
cheetah
crocodile
elephant
giraffe
leopard
lion
rhinoceros
warthog
zebra

y	h	l	a	r	l	r	q	r	w
r	t	c	h	e	e	t	a	h	a
i	x	a	l	i	o	n	z	i	r
a	b	e	l	e	p	h	a	n	t
c	z	e	b	r	a	t	u	o	h
f	b	f	l	r	r	o	o	c	o
c	r	o	c	o	d	i	l	e	g
g	i	r	a	f	f	e	y	r	y
p	r	b	u	f	f	a	l	o	a
p	i	o	t	h	v	s	t	s	t

SPOTTED HYENAS are also known as **LAUGHING HYENAS,** because they **CACKLE LOUDLY** to communicate.

◀ GIRAFFE

MATCH GAME

Match the mind-boggling magnifications below to the safari animals on the right-hand page.

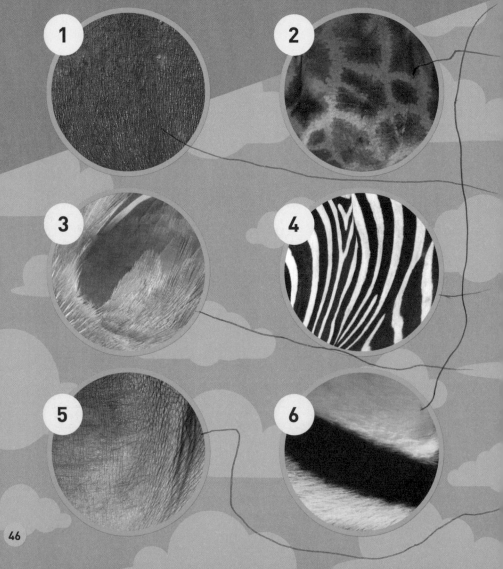

1

2

3

4

5

6

Gazelle

Giraffe

A

B

Hippo

Rhino

C

D

Roller

Zebra

E

F

47

QUIZ WHIZ

Do you know the answers to the safari animal questions below?

1. Which animal is famous for being striped?
   - a. Zebra
   - b. Bear
   - c. Lion

2. How long is a giraffe's tongue?
   - a. 2 inches (5 cm)
   - b. 20 inches (51 cm)
   - c. 35 inches (90 cm)

3. What is a male elephant called?
   - a. Buck
   - b. Boar
   - c. Bull

4. Which safari animal is known for its "laugh"?
   - a. Spotted tiger
   - b. Spotted hyena
   - c. Spotted warthog

5. How many species of baboons are there?
   - a. One
   - b. Five
   - c. Nine

6. African wild dogs are:
   - a. Canines
   - b. Felines
   - c. Reptiles

7. A gazelle is a type of:
   - a. Antelope
   - b. Ant
   - c. Elephant

8. Which animal name rhymes with the word "smile"?
   - a. Lion
   - b. Zebra
   - c. Crocodile

9. Unlike other big cats, which animal hunts mainly during the day?
   - a. Lion
   - b. Leopard
   - c. Cheetah

10. Warthog tusks can grow up to approximately how long?
    - a. 10 inches (25 cm)
    - b. 30 inches (75 cm)
    - c. 37 inches (95 cm)

ELEPHANT ▶

MAZE

Help the gazelle through the maze.

WORD WHEELS

Can you unscramble
the safari animals
in the two word wheels?

ON THE FARM

Read on for **FUN FACTS** and **PUZZLES** from down on the farm.

A COW'S STOMACH is **DIVIDED INTO FOUR CHAMBERS**, allowing it to **DIGEST GRASS** and **GRAINS** better.

CROSSWORDS

Fill in the crosswords by solving the cryptic clues below.

Can you work out the farm code word using the letters in the shaded squares?

The **CHICKEN** is the **CLOSEST** living **RELATIVE** to the **TYRANNOSAURUS REX.**

ACROSS
1 Very impressive or incredible
5 Type of vehicle
7 Illustration; typical case
8 Frequent
11 The whole of
12 Crisis

DOWN
2 Zero
3 Stumble
4 Cautiously
6 Furniture item with a flat top
9 Donate
10 Drizzle, perhaps

GOAT ▶

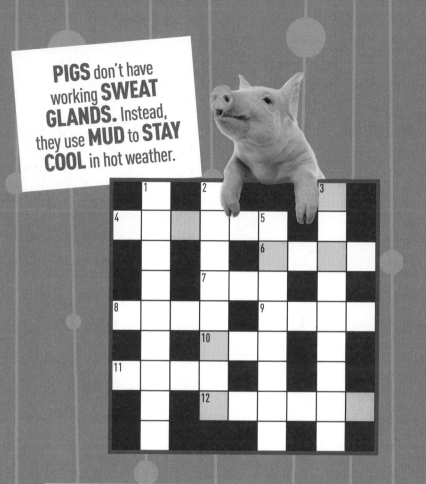

PIGS don't have working **SWEAT GLANDS.** Instead, they use **MUD** to **STAY COOL** in hot weather.

ACROSS
4 Country
6 A single time
7 Possess
8 Animals that moo
9 Large white waterbird
10 A large primate
11 List of food items at a restaurant
12 Outcome

DOWN
1 Trick-or-treating happens on this day
2 *Tyrannosaurus rex,* for example
3 Shape with four sides
5 Something impossible to understand

SUDOKU

Help the farm animals solve the sudoku.

Fill in the blank squares so that numbers 1 to 6 appear once in each row, column, and 3x2 box.

3	1	5			
4				6	3
2	3		6		
5		6		3	2
1	2				
6			4		

Only **FEMALE DUCKS** actually **"QUACK,"** but all ducks **GRUNT, YODEL,** and **WHISTLE.**

Puzzle 1

4	3	6		5	2
		1			
			5		4
1		5			
			3		
2				6	5

Puzzle 2

4	2	5	3	1	
					5
	4		6		
		3		2	
2					
	5	1		6	2

A group of **GEESE** can be called a **"GAGGLE"** on the ground, a **"SKEIN"** in flight, and a **"FLOCK"** anywhere.

MATCH GAME

Match the mind-boggling magnifications below to the named pictures on the right-hand page.

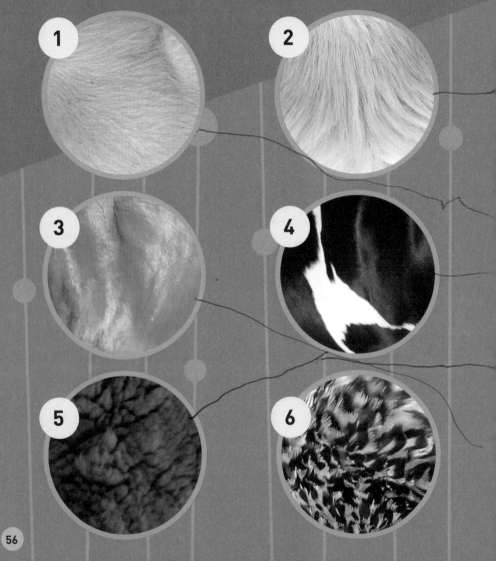

Goat

A

Duck

B

Cow

C

Sheep

D

Pig

E

F

Horse

QUIZ WHIZ

Do you know the answers to the farm animal questions below?

1. Which animal is well-known for its loud morning call?
   a. Rooster
   b. Sheep
   c. Cow

2. A group of geese is called a:
   a. Pack
   b. Skein
   c. Herd

3. Which animal grazes in a flock?
   a. Sheep
   b. Rabbit
   c. Dog

4. Which bird lays eggs and lives in a coop?
   a. Chicken
   b. Swan
   c. Parrot

5. Which animal helps to herd and control sheep?
   a. Dog
   b. Cat
   c. Pig

6. Horses sleep in a:
   a. Farmhouse
   b. Coop
   c. Stable

7. Farmers shear wool from:
   a. Horses
   b. Chickens
   c. Sheep

8. A baby cow is called a:
   a. Cub
   b. Calf
   c. Piglet

9. A young sheep is called a:
   a. Kitten
   b. Puppy
   c. Lamb

10. A female donkey is called a:
    a. Jenny
    b. Jackie
    c. Joyce

BORDER COLLIE ▶

Help the hen around the maze to reach her chick.

WORD WHEELS

Can you unscramble the farm animals in the two word wheels?

Left wheel: R B A I B T

Right wheel: K N E Y D O

CURIOUS
CREATURES

Eager to learn more about our fascinating friends? Read on for **FUN FACTS** and **PUZZLES** about odd animals.

TARSIERS have the nickname **"FOREST GOBLINS"** because of their **TINY SIZE** and **FUNNY APPEARANCE.**

CROSSWORDS

Fill in the crosswords by solving the cryptic clues below.

Can you work out the curious creature code word using the letters in the shaded squares?

Each **MEERKAT MOB** has at least one **SENTRY** that **STANDS UP ON ITS HIND LEGS** to look out for danger.

ACROSS
4 Very clever or talented
6 Adult males
8 Large number of people
9 Tube you can drink through
10 Crafty and cunning
12 Place in a school where lessons take place

DOWN
1 Opposite of false
2 The direction the hands move on a watch
3 Very well known
5 This comes after yesterday and before tomorrow
6 Melodic sounds
7 Ordinary; regular
11 Big cat that roars

A MALE GHARIAL uses the LUMP at the end of its THIN SNOUT to BLOW BUBBLES and ATTRACT FEMALES.

ACROSS

4 Thrill
6 The opposite of win
7 Too
8 Remove the skin from a fruit
9 Where you are right now
10 What an airplane takes off from

DOWN

1 Very good
2 Find or locate
3 The day before today
5 Large mammal with a trunk

MANTIS SHRIMP ▶

63

SUDOKU

Help the curious creatures solve the sudoku.

Fill in the blank squares so that numbers 1 to 6 appear once in each row, column, and 3x2 box.

4		6	3		1
				5	
	4		2		3
6		2		4	
	6				
3			4		

GERENUKS are sometimes called **"GIRAFFE GAZELLES"** because of their **LONG, THIN NECKS.**

LOWLAND STREAKED TENRECS, native to **MADAGASCAR,** rub their spines together to **COMMUNICATE.**

Puzzle 1 (6×6):

				1	2
			4	3	6
6	2				5
4					
5	3	2			
1	4				

Puzzle 2 (6×6):

5		4			1
	3	2			
		3			
			5		4
			6	4	3
3			2		5

WORD SEARCHES

Can you find these animal words?

Search left to right and up and down to find the words listed in the boxes below.

n	t	z	p	z	a	s	g	t	s
h	e	r	m	i	t	c	r	a	b
a	o	i	n	x	s	o	r	r	f
n	s	h	a	r	k	r	u	a	i
t	p	o	r	c	u	p	i	n	e
e	o	t	l	u	n	i	v	t	e
a	n	t	t	j	k	o	l	u	y
t	g	e	o	q	h	n	a	l	s
e	e	r	v	s	r	c	s	a	r
r	n	m	m	o	l	e	e	s	j

Known for being **PRICKLY, PORCUPINES** are first born with **SOFT SPIKES,** which harden over a few days.

anteater
hermit crab
mole
otter
porcupine
scorpion
shark
skunk
sponge
tarantula

◄ TAMANDUA

Despite being **LARGE, HAIRY,** and **SCARY-LOOKING, TARANTULAS** are usually **HARMLESS TO HUMANS.**

chameleon

dolphin

lemur

meerkat

ostrich

owl

panda

peacock

penguin

wolf

COLUGOS are forest-dwelling animals that live in **ASIA.** Flaps of skin between their legs allow them to **GLIDE** as they **LEAP** between trees.

u	h	r	f	i	t	r	e	z	m
a	t	b	s	n	h	q	l	p	b
v	h	a	x	a	i	m	n	e	s
o	d	d	a	v	t	q	p	n	o
w	o	l	f	a	k	e	e	g	i
l	l	e	m	u	r	a	a	u	b
g	p	a	n	d	a	a	c	i	s
c	h	a	m	e	l	e	o	n	q
l	i	o	s	t	r	i	c	h	t
l	n	p	m	e	e	r	k	a	t

QUIZ WHIZ

1. Which animal has the ability to change color?
   a. Chameleon
   b. Tarantula
   c. Panda

2. On which island do you find lemurs in the wild?
   a. Madagascar
   b. Iceland
   c. Ireland

3. Why do stick insects resemble sticks?
   a. To attract a mate
   b. To make it hard for predators to detect them
   c. To keep cool

4. What is a porcupine particularly known for?
   a. Its big teeth
   b. Its sharp spines
   c. Its orange eyes

5. How does a skunk defend itself from predators?
   a. Emits a foul-smelling spray
   b. Jumps up and down
   c. Hides in a shell

6. How do anteaters feed on small insects?
   a. Using their sticky tongues
   b. Scooping them up in their large paws
   c. Sweeping them up with their tails

7. Roughly, how many species of tarantula are known to exist?
   a. 8
   b. 80
   c. 800

8. How long can an otter remain underwater?
   a. Up to four seconds
   b. Up to four minutes
   c. Up to forty minutes

9. What do pandas feed on almost entirely?
   a. Oats
   b. Worms
   c. Bamboo

10. Meerkats prefer to live:
    a. Alone
    b. In groups
    c. In pairs

PANDA ▶

MAZE

Help the jerboa hop through the maze.

Although **AXOLOTL** are known as **"WALKING FISH,"** they are actually **AMPHIBIANS.**

WORD WHEELS

Can you unscramble the curious creatures in the two word wheels?

IN THE
WATER

Dive in and discover **FUN FACTS** and **PUZZLES** from under the water.

DOLPHINS COMMUNICATE in lots of different ways, including **BODY LANGUAGE, WHISTLES,** and **SQUEAKS.**

CROSSWORDS

Fill in the crosswords by solving the cryptic clues below.

Can you work out the sea animal code word using the letters in the shaded squares?

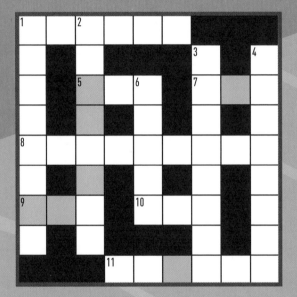

SEA STARS, commonly called **"STARFISH,"** aren't really fish! They belong to the same family as **SEA URCHINS** and **SPONGES.**

ACROSS
1 Hug
5 2 + 3, for instance
7 Road vehicle
8 Bright flash that is followed by thunder
9 Observe with your eyes
10 Tell an untruth
11 A young cat

DOWN
1 Not giving enough attention to a task
2 Have a different opinion from another
3 Chance event that may lead to injury
4 Scare
6 Gold or iron, for instance

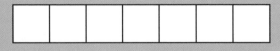

SEA LIONS are **QUICK!** They can reach **SPEEDS** up to **25 MILES** (40 km) **AN HOUR.**

An **OCTOPUS** can use its **EIGHT STRONG ARMS** to build itself a den, complete with a closable **ROCK "DOOR."**

ACROSS
1 Length of space between two points
5 You hear with this
6 Polar ___ : powerful arctic animals
7 Completely confuses
10 Female monarch
11 Rodent with a long tail
12 Jointly

DOWN
2 Small mammal that is mouse-like and has a long snout
3 Emergency vehicle
4 Mistake
8 What an active volcano might do
9 Planet we live on

SUDOKU

Help the sea animals solve the sudoku.

Fill in the blank squares so that numbers 1 to 6 appear once in each row, column, and 3x2 box.

CLOWNFISH

Thanks to their **POWERFUL TAILS, GREAT WHITE SHARKS** can **SWIM** at up to **35 MILES** (56 KM) **AN HOUR!**

3	5		4		
2		6	3	1	
	1		6	4	2
		1		2	4

WORD SEARCHES

Can you find the sea animal words?

Search left to right and up and down to find the words listed in the boxes below.

PIRANHA
▼

coral
jellyfish
octopus
salmon
sardine

seahorse
seaweed
squid
starfish
trout

o	t	r	s	q	u	i	d	k	f
j	s	t	a	r	f	i	s	h	t
j	e	l	l	y	f	i	s	h	u
s	a	r	d	i	n	e	m	u	a
a	h	q	g	x	i	b	r	w	p
l	o	c	t	o	p	u	s	b	o
m	r	r	t	r	o	u	t	t	p
o	s	e	a	w	e	e	d	s	t
n	e	l	l	s	j	h	l	e	h
x	i	u	z	r	c	o	r	a	l

Though **FEMALE SEAHORSES LAY THE EGGS,** it's the males that actually carry them and **GIVE BIRTH.**

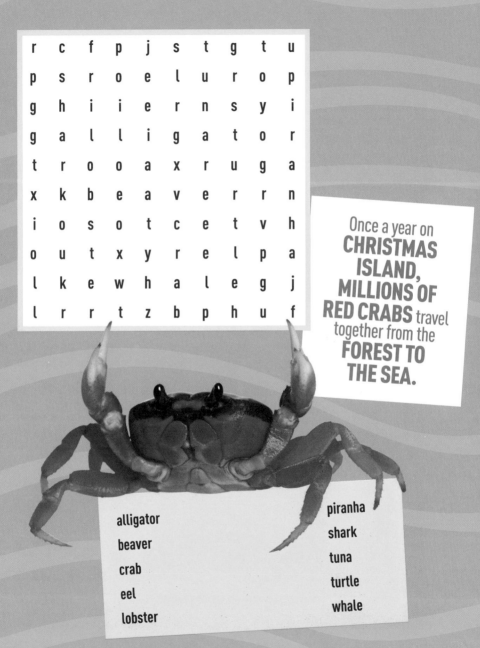

r	c	f	p	j	s	t	g	t	u
p	s	r	o	e	l	u	r	o	p
g	h	i	i	e	r	n	s	y	i
g	a	l	l	i	g	a	t	o	r
t	r	o	o	a	x	r	u	g	a
x	k	b	e	a	v	e	r	r	n
i	o	s	o	t	c	e	t	v	h
o	u	t	x	y	r	e	l	p	a
l	k	e	w	h	a	l	e	g	j
l	r	r	t	z	b	p	h	u	f

Once a year on **CHRISTMAS ISLAND, MILLIONS OF RED CRABS** travel together from the **FOREST TO THE SEA.**

alligator
beaver
crab
eel
lobster

piranha
shark
tuna
turtle
whale

SPOT THE DIFFERENCE

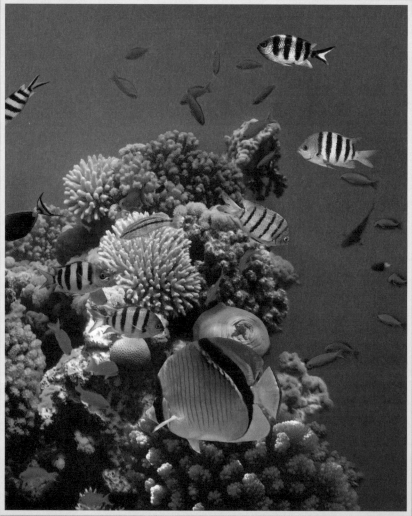

Compare the two images of a coral reef.
Can you spot the five differences
between the images?

QUIZ WHIZ

Do you know the answers to the water animal questions below?

1. How fast can the great white shark swim?
   a. 35 mph (56 km/h)
   b. 10 mph (16 km/h)
   c. 50 mph (80 km/h)

2. How many arms does an octopus have?
   a. Four
   b. Six
   c. Eight

3. The giant squid can grow as long as:
   a. 7 feet (2 m)
   b. 16 feet (5 m)
   c. 43 feet (13 m)

4. How many arms can a starfish have?
   a. Two
   b. Five
   c. Four

5. What type of creature is a turtle?
   a. Amphibian
   b. Mammal
   c. Reptile

6. A great white shark can grow up to approximately what length?
   a. 3 feet (1 m)
   b. 20 feet (6 m)
   c. 65 feet (20 m)

7. Which of these is a small tropical fish?
   a. Clownfish
   b. Magicianfish
   c. Builderfish

8. How many legs do crabs have?
   a. Four
   b. Six
   c. Ten

9. What type of creature is a dolphin?
   a. Amphibian
   b. Mammal
   c. Reptile

10. If threatened, a squid might:
    a. Make loud noises
    b. Grow in size
    c. Squirt ink

ORCA ▶

MAZE

Help the penguin around the maze until it finds the exit.

WORD WHEELS

Can you unscramble the water animals in the two word wheels?

Word wheel 1: A E B R E V (center: V)

Word wheel 2: R P O E P O I S (center: P)

SOLUTIONS

CROSSWORDS 8–9

Crossword 1:

D	A	I	S	I	E	S		S
I				N		A		U
F		T		C	R	U	M	B
F		Y		O		S		S
I	M	P	O	R	T	A	N	T
C		I		R		G		A
U	N	C	L	E		E		N
L		A		C				C
T		L	E	T	T	U	C	E

Code word: TIGER

Crossword 2:

C	H	E	R	R	Y				
U		N		U		R			I
S	E	V	E	N	T	E	E	N	
T		E				L		T	
O	W	L	S		M	A	K	E	
M		O				T		R	
E	X	P	E	N	S	I	V	E	
R		E		U		V		S	
		S	T	R	E	E	T		

Code word: PANTHER

SUDOKU 10–11

Sudoku 1:

3	6	5	2	1	4
4	1	2	5	6	3
2	3	1	6	4	5
5	4	6	1	3	2
1	2	4	3	5	6
6	5	3	4	2	1

Sudoku 2:

4	3	6	1	5	2
5	2	1	6	4	3
3	6	2	5	1	4
1	4	5	2	3	6
6	5	4	3	2	1
2	1	3	4	6	5

Sudoku 3:

4	2	5	3	1	6
1	3	6	2	4	5
5	4	2	6	3	1
6	1	3	5	2	4
2	6	4	1	5	3
3	5	1	4	6	2

WORD SEARCHES 12–13

Word Search 1:

```
e k e s u w g f e s
x d a g j a g u a r
o a w s p s p o t s
o p u m a t r l r e
y l i o n r a e e l
u a k t t i r o a r
z z k o h p t p s s
s v c h e e t a h a
t i g e r s a r w e
a x b p l j i d c s
```

Word Search 2:

```
w a u x l m u p b g
r q c o u g a r s h
a g a t a t s p g g
o p r e d a t o r t
p r n e s c e u i s
t e i t o l a n c a
i y v h w a l c z r
t l o f m w t e m o
c y r u d s h i h r
f i e r c e a w i a
```

82

QUIZ WHIZ 14

1. b – Lion
2. c – Spots
3. a – Puma
4. b – Cheetah
5. c – To help distribute their weight when walking on snow
6. b – Liger
7. c – Tiger
8. c – Pride
9. a – Dense rainforest
10. b – 5 miles (8 k) away

MAZE 15

WORD WHEELS 15

Cheetah
Jaguar

SOLUTIONS

CROSSWORDS 18–19

Crossword 1 grid:

B	R	E	A	K	F	A	S	T
E					O			O
D	E	S	S	E	R	T		E
S			P		G			S
	B	E	E	H	I	V	E	
P		C		V			T	
U		V	I	N	E	G	A	R
M		A					R	E
A	P	O	L	O	G	I	Z	E

Code word: PARROT

Crossword 2 grid:

	C	A	R	R	O	T	S		
P		M				E			W
U	N	P	O	P	U	L	A	R
S		H		E		E			I
H		I		A		S			T
I		B		C		C			E
N	E	I	G	H	B	O	R	
G		A				P		
	A	N	O	T	H	E	R	

Code word: SLOTH

SUDOKU 20–21

Sudoku 1:

3	6	1	4	2	5
2	4	5	6	1	3
5	1	3	2	4	6
6	2	4	3	5	1
1	3	2	5	6	4
4	5	6	1	3	2

Sudoku 2:

3	5	1	4	6	2
2	6	4	3	1	5
5	3	6	1	2	4
4	1	2	6	5	3
6	2	3	5	4	1
1	4	5	2	3	6

Sudoku 3:

3	4	5	1	2	6
1	2	6	3	4	5
5	1	2	6	3	4
6	3	4	5	1	2
2	6	1	4	5	3
4	5	3	2	6	1

WORD SEARCHES 22–23

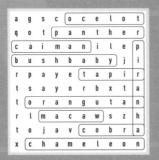

Word search 1:

a	g	s	c	o	c	e	l	o	t
q	o	t	p	a	n	t	h	e	r
c	a	i	m	a	n	i	l	e	p
b	u	s	h	b	a	b	y	j	i
r	p	a	y	e	t	a	p	i	r
t	s	a	y	n	r	b	x	t	a
t	o	r	a	n	g	u	t	a	n
r	l	m	a	c	a	w	s	z	h
t	o	j	a	v	c	o	b	r	a
x	c	h	a	m	e	l	e	o	n

Word search 2:

i	m	b	a	t	o	u	c	a	n
l	l	a	x	p	h	m	h	g	e
m	v	a	e	y	i	p	i	o	n
q	y	o	l	t	x	x	m	r	t
q	t	p	q	h	u	o	p	i	d
a	n	a	c	o	n	d	a	l	u
s	l	r	f	n	a	r	n	l	o
y	f	r	o	g	a	r	z	a	a
s	l	o	t	h	i	s	e	i	p
i	s	t	f	o	e	i	e	p	s

SOLUTIONS

CROSSWORDS 28–29

Crossword 1:
```
D I R E C T
E   E     T     I
C   C U B   R A N
E   O   E   I     T
M A R M A L A D E
B   D   R   N     R
E Y E   D O G   N
R   R     L     E
      N E W E S T
```
Code word: CROCODILE

Crossword 2:
```
B L U N D E R S
    N   I     T
O D D   S T E A M
    E   A     I
A I R   P L A N E
    C   P   G
G E E S E   A G E
        A     I
    E N T R A N C E
```
Code word: OTTER

SUDOKU 30–31

5	4	1	6	3	2
6	2	3	5	4	1
4	1	6	2	5	3
2	3	5	1	6	4
3	5	2	4	1	6
1	6	4	3	2	5

2	5	4	3	1	6
3	6	1	4	5	2
6	3	5	1	2	4
1	4	2	5	6	3
5	2	3	6	4	1
4	1	6	2	3	5

5	1	3	6	4	2
2	4	6	3	5	1
6	5	4	2	1	3
1	3	2	4	6	5
4	2	5	1	3	6
3	6	1	5	2	4

WORD SEARCHES 32–33

Word search 1:
```
l p u c r a n e h e
o m a r s h r u d p
j x m o n e l a r x
t i a c a t c r a b
u b b o k f r o g g
z i v d e k e r o o
d j l i z a r d n t
v r d l a l l o f t
u c b e t u r t l e
p t w d g t s k y r
```

Word search 2:
```
l y a b u r t w c s
m r d e h y b w r h
a z u a e l h a r
n e c v r l a c y f
g c k e o a c p f i
r a s r n m k f r s
o i i g a i b r s h
v e m l u i n e a y
e a l l i g a t o r
u n t s q o r c q e
```

SPOT THE DIFFERENCE 34–35

QUIZ WHIZ 36

1. a – Anaconda
2. a – Crane
3. c – Mallard
4. b – Building dams
5. c – Rat
6. c – Crab
7. b – To lay eggs
8. a – Bog
9. a – Water lily
10. a – Tadpole

MAZE 37

WORD WHEELS 37

Alligator
Turtle

SOLUTIONS

CROSSWORDS 40–41

First crossword:

	A	C	R	O	B	A	T	
H		E			L		E	
E	E	L		R	L		N	
X		E	V	E	N	I	N	G
A		B		P		G		L
G	O	R	I	L	L	A		A
O		A		Y		T	E	N
N		T				O		D
	L	E	O	P	A	R	D	

Code word: ELEPHANT

Second crossword:

D	E	C	R	E	A	S	E	
E		H			U		C	
C	H	O	S	E	B		O	
I		C		L	E	M	O	N
S		O		B		A		S
I	G	L	O	O		R		I
O		A		W	E	I	R	D
N		T				N		E
	R	E	I	N	D	E	E	R

Code word: CHEETAH

SUDOKU 42–43

2	3	5	6	4	1
1	4	6	3	5	2
3	5	1	2	6	4
4	6	2	1	3	5
6	1	4	5	2	3
5	2	3	4	1	6

5	3	4	1	6	2
2	1	6	5	3	4
1	4	5	6	2	3
3	6	2	4	1	5
4	2	1	3	5	6
6	5	3	2	4	1

4	1	5	3	6	2
3	6	2	4	1	5
6	2	4	1	5	3
1	5	3	2	4	6
2	4	6	5	3	1
5	3	1	6	2	4

WORD SEARCHES 44–45

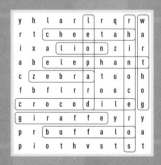

MATCH GAME

1 – C Hippo
2 – B Giraffe
3 – E Roller

4 – F Zebra
5 – D Rhino
6 – A Gazelle

QUIZ WHIZ

1. a – Zebra
2. b – 20 inches (51 cm)
3. c – Bull
4. b – Spotted hyena
5. b – Five

6. a – Canines
7. a – Antelope
8. c – Crocodile
9. c – Cheetah
10. a– 10 inches (25 cm)

MAZE

WORD WHEELS

Buffalo
Gazelle

SOLUTIONS

CROSSWORDS 52–53

Code word: FARMER

Code word: TRACTOR

SUDOKU 54–55

3	6	5	2	1	4
4	1	2	5	6	3
2	3	1	6	4	5
5	4	6	1	3	2
1	2	4	3	5	6
6	5	3	4	2	1

4	3	6	1	5	2
5	2	1	6	4	3
3	6	2	5	1	4
1	4	5	2	3	6
6	5	4	3	2	1
2	1	3	4	6	5

4	2	5	3	1	6
1	3	6	2	4	5
5	4	2	6	3	1
6	1	3	5	2	4
2	6	4	1	5	3
3	5	1	4	6	2

MATCH GAME 56–57

1 – E Pig

2 – A Goat

3 – F Horse

4 – C Cow

5 – D Sheep

6 – B Duck

QUIZ WHIZ 58

1. a – Rooster
2. b – Skein
3. a – Sheep
4. a – Chicken
5. a – Dog
6. c – Stable
7. c – Sheep
8. b – Calf
9. c – Lamb
10. a– Jenny

MAZE 59

WORD WHEELS 59

Rabbit
Donkey

SOLUTIONS

CROSSWORDS   62-63

Crossword 1:

	T		C		F				Y	
B	R	I	L	L	I	A	N	T		
	U		O		M			O		
M	E	N		C	R	O	W	D		
U		O		K		U		A		
S	T	R	A	W		S	L	Y		
I		M		I		L				
C	L	A	S	S	R	O	O	M		
		L		E			N			

Code word: MEERKAT

Crossword 2:

	E		D				Y		
E	X	C	I	T	E		E		
	C		S		L	O	S	E	
	E		S		E		T		
A	L	S	O		P	E	E	L	
	L		V		H		R		
H	E	R	E		A		D		
	N		R	U	N	W	A	Y	
	T				T		Y		

Code word: OSTRICH

SUDOKU 64-65

4	5	6	3	2	1
2	1	3	6	5	4
5	4	1	2	6	3
6	3	2	1	4	5
1	6	4	5	3	2
3	2	5	4	1	6

3	6	4	5	1	2
2	1	5	4	3	6
6	2	1	3	4	5
4	5	3	6	2	1
5	3	2	1	6	4
1	4	6	2	5	3

5	6	4	3	2	1
1	3	2	4	5	6
4	5	3	1	6	2
6	2	1	5	3	4
2	1	5	6	4	3
3	4	6	2	1	5

WORD SEARCHES 66-67

Word Search 1:

n	t	z	p	z	a	s	g	t	s
h	e	r	m	i	t	c	r	a	b
a	o	i	n	x	s	o	r	r	f
n	s	h	a	r	k	r	u	a	i
t	p	o	r	c	u	p	i	n	e
e	o	t	l	u	n	i	v	t	e
a	n	t	j	k	o	l	u	y	
t	g	e	o	q	h	n	a	l	s
e	e	r	v	s	r	c	s	a	r
r	n	m	m	o	l	e	s	e	j

Word Search 2:

u	h	r	f	i	t	r	e	z	m
a	t	b	s	n	h	q	l	p	b
v	h	a	x	a	i	m	n	e	s
o	d	d	a	v	t	q	p	n	o
w	o	l	f	a	k	e	e	g	i
l	l	e	m	u	r	a	a	u	b
g	p	a	n	d	a	a	c	i	s
c	h	a	m	e	l	e	o	n	q
l	i	o	s	t	r	i	c	h	t
l	n	p	m	e	e	r	k	a	t

92

QUIZ WHIZ

1. a – Chameleon
2. a – Madagascar
3. b – To make it hard for predators to detect them
4. b – Its sharp spines
5. a – Emits a foul-smelling spray
6. a – Using their sticky tongues
7. c – 800
8. b – Up to four minutes
9. c – Bamboo
10. b – In groups

MAZE

WORD WHEELS

Dolphin
Penguin

SOLUTIONS

CROSSWORDS 72–73

```
C U D D L E           E
A     I           A       F
R   S U M       C A R
E   A   E       C       I
L I G H T N I N G
E   R   A       D       H
S E E   L I E       T
S   E               N       E
    K I T T E N
```

Code word: SEA STAR

```
D I S T A N C E       E
    H       M               R
E A R       B E A R S
    E       U               O
B E W I L D E R S
    R       A               A
Q U E E N       R A T
    P       C               T
T O G E T H E R
```

Code word: OCTOPUS

SUDOKU 74–75

```
1 6 4 2 5 3
3 5 2 4 6 1
2 4 6 3 1 5
5 1 3 6 4 2
6 3 1 5 2 4
4 2 5 1 3 6
```

```
5 3 1 6 2 4
4 6 2 1 5 3
2 5 4 3 1 6
6 1 3 5 4 2
1 4 6 2 3 5
3 2 5 4 6 1
```

```
6 1 2 3 4 5
3 5 4 1 6 2
1 2 3 4 5 6
5 4 6 2 3 1
4 6 1 5 2 3
2 3 5 6 1 4
```

WORD SEARCHES 76–77

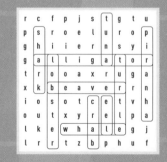

```
o t r s q u i d k f
j s t a r f i s h t
j e l l y f i s h u
s a r d i n e m u a
a h q g x i b r w p
l o c t o p u s b o
m r r t r o u t t p
o s e a w e e d s t
n e l l s j h l e h
x i u z r c o r a l
```

```
r c f p j s t g t u
p s r o e l u r o p
g h i i e r n s y i
g a l l i g a t o r
t r o o a x r u g a
x k b e a v e r r n
i o s o t c e t v h
o u t x y r e l p a
l k e w h a l e g j
l r r t z b p h u f
```

SPOT THE DIFFERENCE 78–79

QUIZ WHIZ 80

1. a – 35 miles (56 km) an hour
2. c – Eight
3. c – 43 feet (13 m)
4. b – Five
5. c – Reptile
6. b – 20 feet (6 m)
7. a – Clownfish
8. c – Ten
9. b – Mammal
10. c – Squirt ink

MAZE 81

WORD WHEELS 81

Beaver
Porpoise

LION vs.
DRAGONFLY?

Think you've solved all the puzzles? Not so fast!
The surprising animal matchups in these books will
show you why a bug can be deadlier than a beast
and so much more!